READY, SET, DRAW!

AIRPLANES AND SHIPS YOU CAN DRAW

Nicole Brecke

Patricia M. Stockland

M Millbrook Press / Minneapolis

The images in this book are used with the permission of: © iStockphoto.com/Dzianis Miraniuk, p. 4; © iStockphoto.com, pp. 4, 5, 19; © iStockphoto.com/Boris Yankov, p. 5; © iStockphoto.com/JR Trice, p. 5; © iStockphoto.com/Rami Ben Ami, p. 7; © iStockphoto.com/Guillermo Perales Gonzalez, p. 9; © iStockphoto.com/Michael Grube, p. 11; © iStockphoto.com/Hendrik De Bruyne, p. 15; © iStockphoto.com/Kert, p. 23; © iStockphoto.com/George Clerk, p. 27; © iStockphoto.com/Allister Clark, p. 31.

Front cover: © iStockphoto.com/Kert (sky); © iStockphoto.com/Rami Ben Ami (water); © iStockphoto.com/blackred (hand).

The publisher wishes to thank Stani V. Bohac, Ph.D., Assistant Research Scientist, Mechanical Engineering, University of Michigan, for serving as a consultant on this title.

Edited by Mari Kesselring

Millbrook Press
A division of Lerner Publishing Group, Inc.
241 First Avenue North
Minneapolis, MN 55401 U.S.A.

Website address: www.lernerbooks.com

Library of Congress Cataloging-in-Publication Data

Brecke, Nicole.
    Airplanes and ships you can draw / by Nicole Brecke and Patricia M. Stockland ; illustrated by Nicole Brecke.
       p.   cm. — (Ready, set, draw!)
    Includes index.
    ISBN: 978-0-7613-4166-6 (lib. bdg. : alk. paper)
    1. Airplanes in art—Juvenile literature. 2. Ships in art—Juvenile literature. 3. Drawing—Technique—Juvenile literature. I. Stockland, Patricia M. II. Title.
    NC825.A4B74 2010
    743'.8629133—dc22   2009023652

Manufactured in the United States of America
1 – BP – 12/15/09

TABLE OF CONTENTS

ABOUT THIS BOOK

Speedboats, jets, and pirate ships! These cool planes and boats will really move you. With the help of this book, you can begin drawing your own transporter. Build a biplane. Or sketch a sub. Soon, you'll know how to create many different airplanes and ships.

Follow these steps to create each airplane or ship. Each drawing begins with a basic form. The form is made up of a line and a couple of shapes. These lines and shapes will help you make your drawing the correct size.

A First, read all the steps and look at the pictures. Then use a pencil to lightly draw the line and shapes shown in RED. You will erase these lines later.

B Next, draw the lines shown in BLUE.

C Keep going! Once you have completed a step, the color of the line changes to BLACK. Follow the BLUE line until you're done.

WHAT YOU WILL NEED

PENCIL SHARPENER

COLORED PENCILS

HELPFUL HINTS

Be creative. Use your imagination. Read about tugboats, helicopters, and 747s. Then follow the steps to sketch your own fleet.

Practice drawing different lines and shapes. All your drawings will start with these.

Use very light pencil lines when you are drawing.

ERASER

Helpful tips and hints will offer you good ideas on making the most of your sketch.

PENCIL

Colors are exciting. Try to use a variety of shades. This will add value, or depth, to your finished drawings.

PAPER

Keep practicing, and have fun!

HOW TO DRAW A SUBMARINE

What is the ultimate underwater spy craft?
A submarine! Militaries have used these sleek, silent vessels for more than one hundred years. The first effective submarine attack happened during the Civil War (1861–1865). The invention of the nuclear-powered submarine in the mid-twentieth century really made the boat famous. Subs are able to launch missiles, carry supplies, send warnings, and scout areas. While underwater, the submarine usually navigates by echolocation, or sound. A submarine dives and surfaces by filling ballast tanks with water or air. Draw your own diving sub.

1 Draw a light, long base oval. Add a center line.

2 Follow the base oval to make an almost-complete hull, or main body. At the opening, draw two vertical lines and a teardrop shape. Finish the sail with two more curved lines.

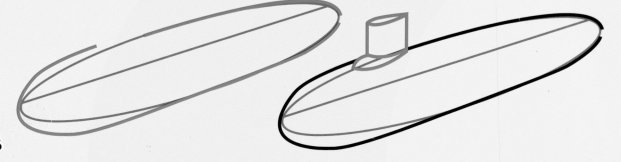

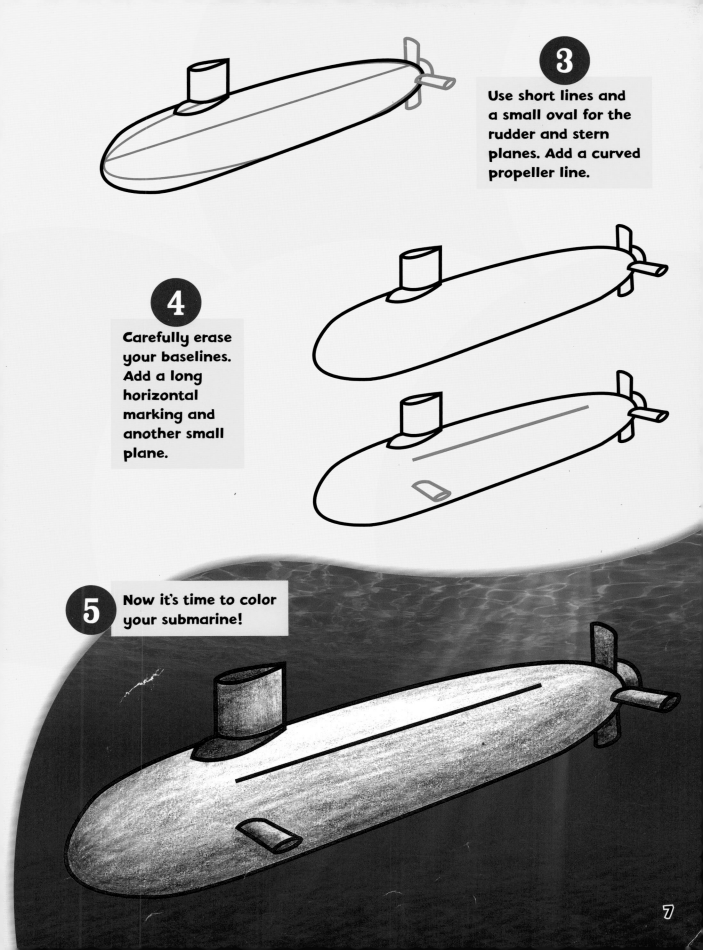

3 Use short lines and a small oval for the rudder and stern planes. Add a curved propeller line.

4 Carefully erase your baselines. Add a long horizontal marking and another small plane.

5 Now it's time to color your submarine!

HOW TO DRAW A FIGHTER JET

Great handling and intense speed make fighter jets amazing aircraft. These military machines have been created to carry weapons and carry out in-air combat. But battling isn't all a fighter jet can do. Sleek designs allow jets to move through the air quickly while remaining less visible to other pilots, ships, and people on the ground. The F-22 Raptor is so fast that it can go supersonic. This means it can travel faster than the speed of sound. Design your own F-22 Raptor!

1

Lightly draw a base square and baseline. Add two curved lines. Draw a curved V shape between these.

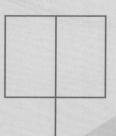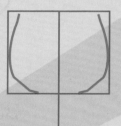

2 Add an angled wing to each side. Use two longer, connected diagonal lines to draw each vertical fin.

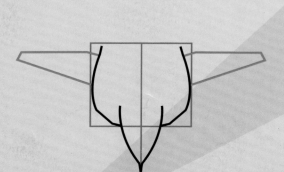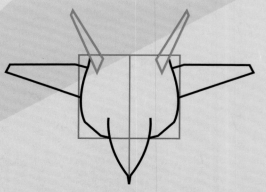

3 Draw a point on each side to make the horizontal fins. Use a dented line to connect the vertical fins. Make a small U shape below the dent. Add an air intake on each side of the nose.

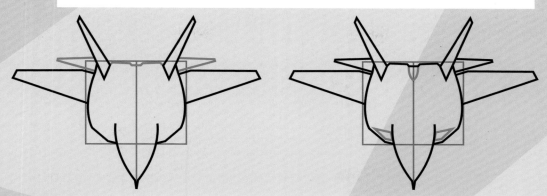

4 Carefully erase your baselines. Draw a crescent shape for the cockpit. Make a curve and two lines below the crescent.

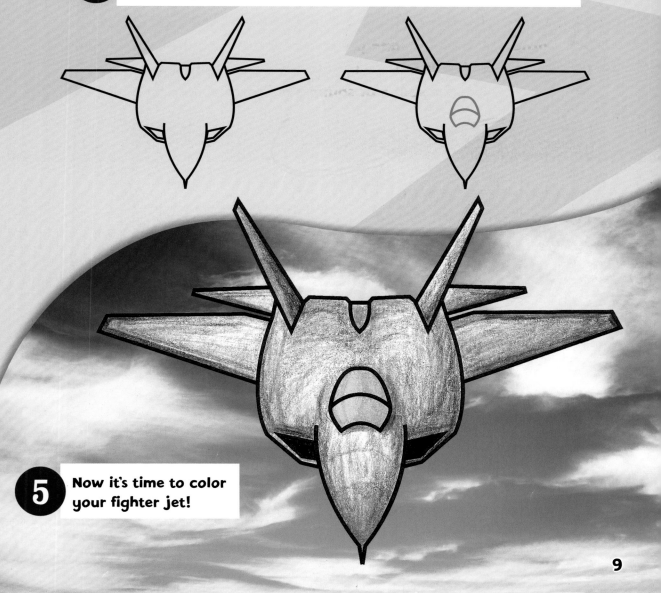

5 Now it's time to color your fighter jet!

HOW TO DRAW A
SPEEDBOAT

Sleek, shiny speedboats might seem like modern machines. But people have been racing these motorboats since the early 1900s. With an oversized hull and a powerful engine, a speedboat is built to move fast. Part of this boat's quickness comes from hydroplaning, or staying above the water. When a speedboat speeds up, most of its hull lifts out of the water. Then the boat easily glides across the surface. How fast will your speedboat go?

1 Draw a long base rectangle. Add a diagonal baseline.

2

In the top half of the rectangle, draw a curving line. Add a longer line below, with a curve that connects to the first. Add a line on top of the baseline. Draw a small rectangle and a short line.

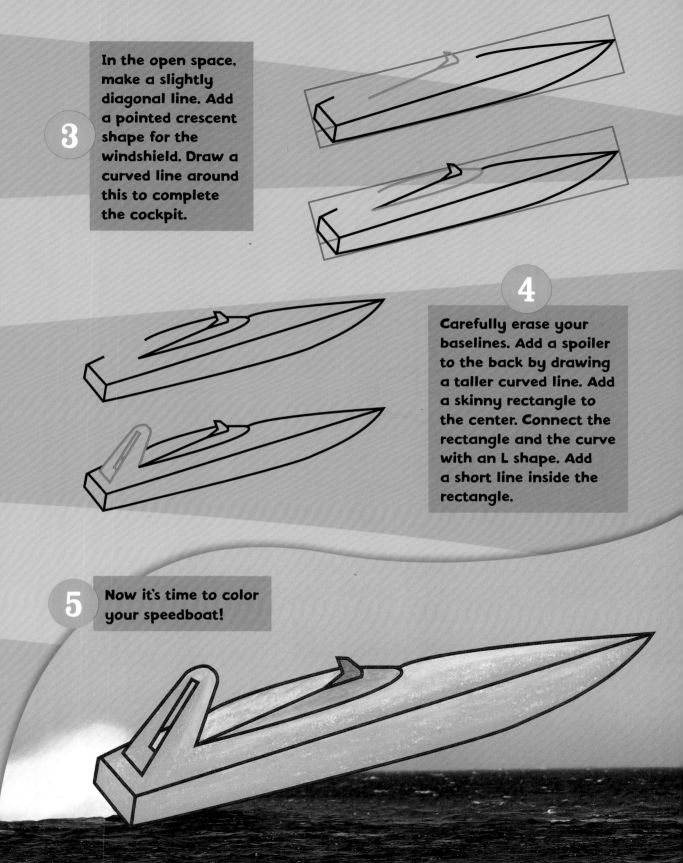

3 In the open space, make a slightly diagonal line. Add a pointed crescent shape for the windshield. Draw a curved line around this to complete the cockpit.

4 Carefully erase your baselines. Add a spoiler to the back by drawing a taller curved line. Add a skinny rectangle to the center. Connect the rectangle and the curve with an L shape. Add a short line inside the rectangle.

5 Now it's time to color your speedboat!

HOW TO DRAW A TUGBOAT

The tugboat is the workhorse of the waterfront. These mighty machines make light work of lugging heavy loads safely into dock. Barges and other larger boats all use tugboats. Their rounded hulls sit deep in the water for extra stability, and their pointy bows help navigate rough seas. Large engines offer lots of power to tugs. Since tugboats do a lot of pulling, their decks are designed for maximum safety. Workers on a tug can move easily around ropes and lines. How much can your tugboat pull?

1 Lightly draw a large base square. Add a center baseline. Make the bow using a thin curved line on the middle of the baseline.

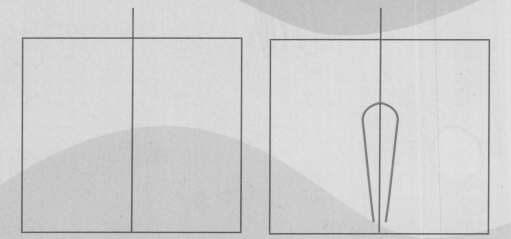

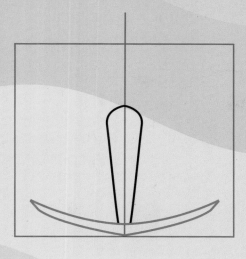

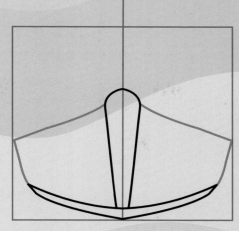

2

Draw two parallel curving lines below the bow. Connect the top of the bow to the bottom of the hull using a bent line on each side.

3

Add two vertical lines. Connect these with a long, skinny oval. Add two more vertical lines and another long, skinny oval.

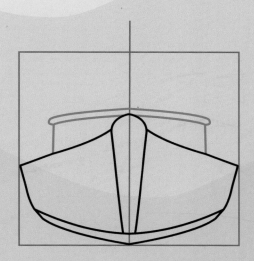

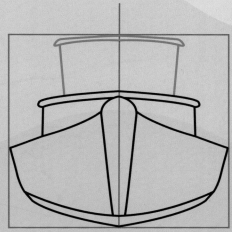

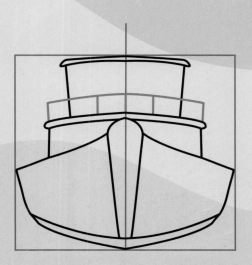

4

Draw five vertical lines and a horizontal line for the rail. Add three rectangles and a short mast.

5 Carefully erase your base shape and line.

6 Add five sets of double circles to the hull.

BOAT BUDDY

Seagulls often feed in waters sailed by tugboats and fly above the decks and docks.

DRAW A SEAGULL!

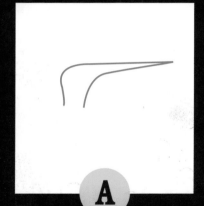

A

B

C

7 Now it's time to
color your tugboat!

THE U.S. COAST GUARD has a Tug Association.
It honors the history of Coast Guard tugboats.

Fly high! The 747 fleet has forever changed air travel. These large commercial airplanes, known as jumbo jets, were created in the late 1960s. About fifty thousand employees of Boeing, an airplane manufacturer, worked on the 747. Airlines have been using them ever since. The modern 747-400 can travel at speeds of nearly 600 miles (966 kilometers) per hour. And the top of the plane's tail is six stories off the ground! A lot of engineering—and parts—go into these large aircraft. Half of a 747-400's six million parts are fasteners. Fly your own jumbo jet!

1

Draw a large base oval and center line. Add a large, slightly angled C shape to the end.

Follow the center line to draw the top of the plane. Add three vertical lines and two short horizontal lines to make the tail.

3 Use two horizontal lines and two small diagonal lines to draw the fin.

4

Draw a wide D shape and a small curved line for the first engine. Make a long curved line connecting to the tail. Add another engine and a short line.

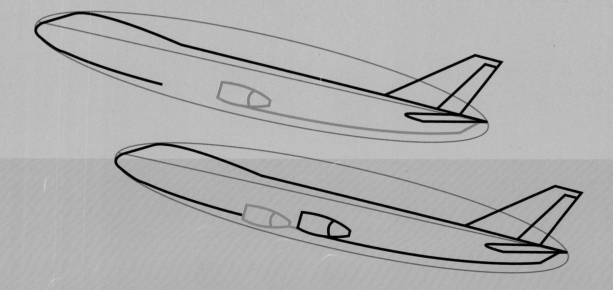

5

Make a long horizontal V shape above the engines for the wing.

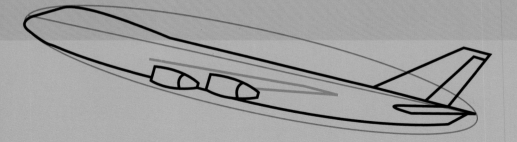

6

Carefully erase your base shape and centerline.

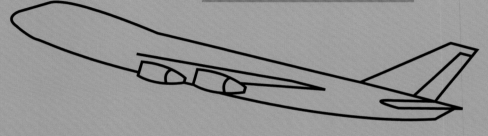

7

Draw a cockpit window and a row of passenger windows. Add five circles and connecting lines for landing gear.

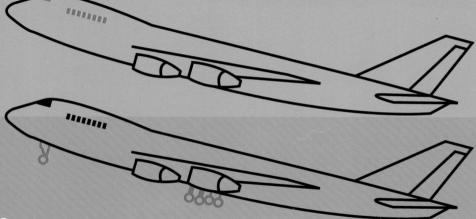

A U.S. postage stamp was made in 1999 to honor the 747.

TRY THIS
Add a colorful stripe to your jumbo jet.

8
Now it's time to color your 747 airplane!

THE FLIGHT DECK of a 747-400 has 365 gauges, lights, and switches. Earlier models had 971!

HOW TO DRAW A BIPLANE

In the early 1900s, the Wright brothers were using a biplane design with the hope of achieving flight. And it worked! The first biplane flew in 1903. By World War I (1914–1918), biplanes had improved and militaries were using aircraft in combat. When planes with single sets of wings proved to be faster, the biplane fell out of favor. But its easy handling is still appreciated. Thanks to a dual pair of wings, the biplane is capable of stunts. Both sporting pilots who do flips and tricks and farmers who use crop dusters fly biplanes.

1

Draw a small base circle and a baseline. Add two more diagonal baselines, parallel to each other.

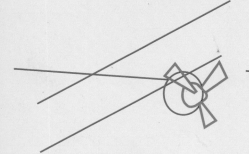

2

Add a cone shape to the circle. Draw three propeller blades. Outline the base circle.

Use a rectangle and a short line to make the first bottom wing. Add three lines for the other wing. Draw a long rectangle for the top. Add two lines between the top and bottom wings.

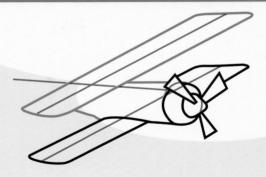

4

Draw an upside-down heart shape for the rudder. Draw a fin on each side. Add two lines to finish the body.

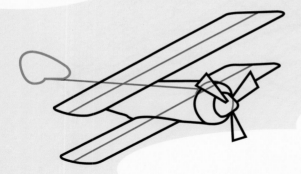

5

Make a pair of double circles for wheels. Draw four diagonal lines to connect the wheels and plane.

6

Carefully erase your baseline and shape.

7

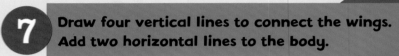

Draw four vertical lines to connect the wings. Add two horizontal lines to the body.

GOOD SIGN

The Wright brothers' 1904 *Flyer* flew a U.S. flag. Biplane pilots often fly fun banners.

DRAW A BANNER!

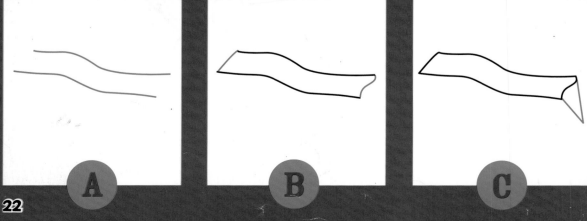

A   B   C

8 Now it's time to color your biplane!

Some biplanes have three or more sets of wings.

HOW TO DRAW A
HELICOPTER

Lift, spin, stability, forward motion. Helicopters are a feat of physics! The idea for these engineering wonders has been around since at least the 1400s. In the early 1920s, pioneering inventors finally created a helicopter that could be used for human flight. Since then, helicopter designs have improved a lot. Traditional airplanes can only fly forward horizontally. But helicopters are capable of vertical flight, or flying straight up. So, pilots are able to steer a "heli" into a spot that might otherwise be unreachable. Helicopters are often used for rescue missions and other challenging situations.

1 Draw a base oval and a baseline. Outline the base oval and part of the baseline, squaring off the bottom left corner.

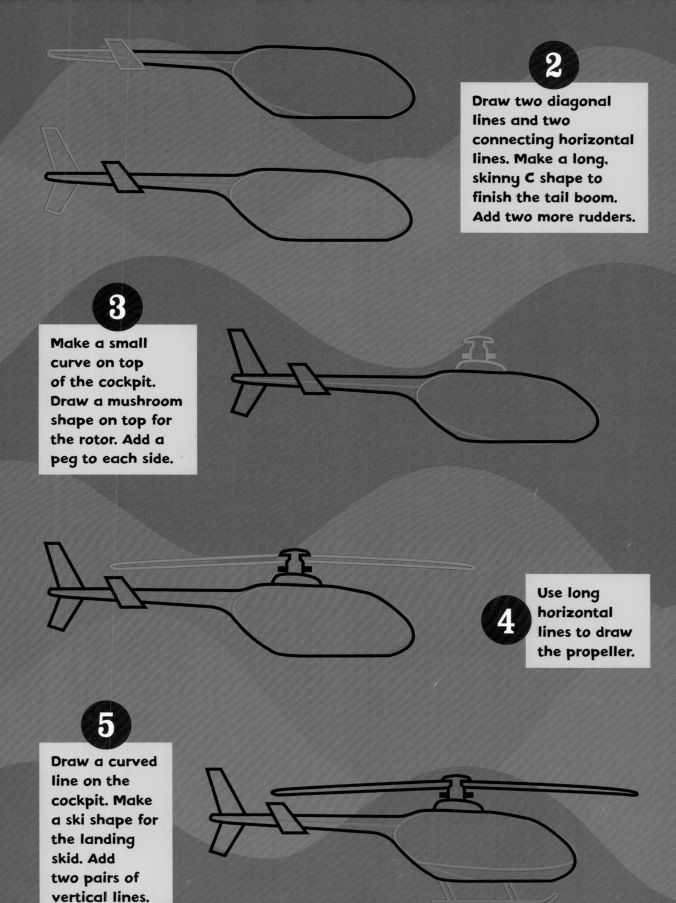

2

Draw two diagonal
lines and two
connecting horizontal
lines. Make a long,
skinny C shape to
finish the tail boom.
Add two more rudders.

3

Make a small
curve on top
of the cockpit.
Draw a mushroom
shape on top for
the rotor. Add a
peg to each side.

4 Use long
horizontal
lines to draw
the propeller.

5

Draw a curved
line on the
cockpit. Make
a ski shape for
the landing
skid. Add
two pairs of
vertical lines.

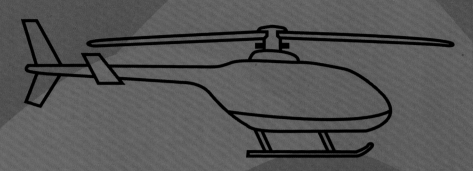

7

Draw a pointed windshield on the front of the cockpit. Add three windows.

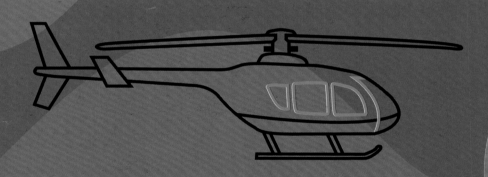

Did you know...
HOSPITALS, RANCHERS, TOURISM BUSINESSES, AND THE ARMED FORCES ALL USE HELICOPTERS.

A helicopter can hover, or stay in one place, in the air.

8 Now it's time to color your helicopter!

HOW TO DRAW A PIRATE SHIP

Avast! It's a pirate ship! These hardy vessels sailed the seas throughout the late 1600s and early 1700s. This time period was the golden age of piracy. Pirate ships had to be strong. Many of the waters they navigated were rough. Pirates in the Caribbean and the western Atlantic Ocean often experienced hurricanes. Pirate ships had special sails for storms as well as strong hulls and sturdy pumps. Pirates whose ships survived storms often raided the wreckage of ships that didn't. The ships also carried armament, or guns and cannons. What does your pirate ship carry?

1 Draw a base rectangle and two baselines, one slightly longer than the other.

2 Draw a pair of curved lines. Below this, make two short lines and one long line. Add another set of curved lines. Add a small V to the front. At the back, draw three lines to finish the hull.

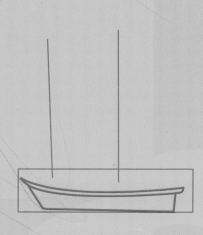

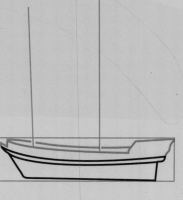

3 Follow the baselines to draw two masts. Add a third set of lines to the front. Use three angled lines to make a large sail on the main mast. Repeat this on the front mast.

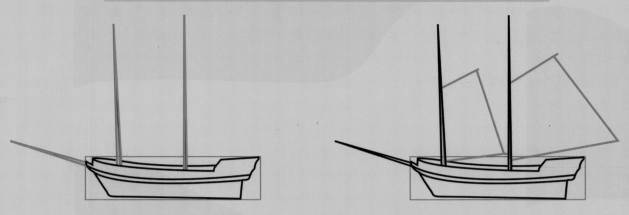

4 Draw a triangle at the top of each mast. Add two angled lines and a curved line to each. Make three jib sails at the front of the ship, using three curved lines for each sail.

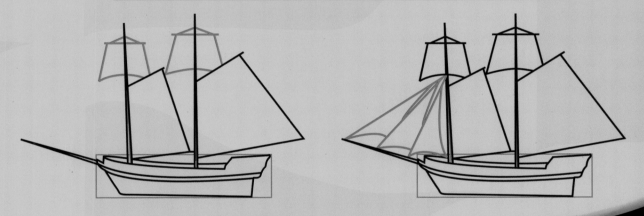

Fast Fact...

PIRATES OFTEN BEACHED THEIR SHIPS TO CLEAN THE HULLS. A SHIP WITH A CLEAN HULL CAN SAIL FASTER.

5 Carefully erase your base shape and lines.

6

Draw ropes among the sails: connect the tip of the jib to the front mast. Draw a horizontal line under each top sail. Make an X shape between the masts.

WARNING FLAG

The familiar pirate flag, with its image of a skull and crossbones, is called the Jolly Roger.

DRAW A SKULL AND CROSSBONES!

A

B

C

TRY THIS
Use darker colors to add
shading to your ship.

 Now it's time to color your pirate ship!

FURTHER READING

Boat Safe Kids
http://www.boatsafe.com/kids/index.htm

Boeing: The Wonder of Flight
http://www.boeing.com/companyoffices/aboutus/wonder_of_flight/index.html

Coppendale, Jean. *Pirates and Ships: Explore Inside*. Philadelphia: Running Press Kids, 2005.

Havercroft, Elizabeth. *A Year on a Pirate Ship*. Minneapolis: Millbrook Press, 2009.

Kentley, Eric. *Eyewitness: Boat*. New York: DK Publishing, 2000.

NOVA: Battle of the X-Planes
http://www.pbs.org/wgbh/nova/xplanes

Oxlade, Chris. *Airplanes Inside and Out*. New York: PowerKids Press, 2009.

INDEX